Take-Home/ Keep-at-Home Books

Out of the Blue

Harcourt Brace & Company

Orlando   Atlanta   Austin   Boston   San Francisco   Chicago   Dallas   New York   Toronto   London

ISBN 0-15-307473-6

10 11 12 13 14 15 16 022 04 03 02 01 00

C O N T E N T S

Grade 2

OUT OF THE BLUE

CELEBRATE ME!

New School, New Friends (This Is the Way We Go to School)

The Case of the Missing Lunch (Emily and Alice Again)

Run-Away Tire (Max Found Two Sticks)

The Best Machine (Dinosaurs Alive and Well!)

WE BELONG TOGETHER

Sisters Forever (Matthew and Tilly)

The Perfect Pet (Mr. Putter and Tabby Pour the Tea)

The Big Sneeze (Six-Dinner Sid)

I Can Go Anyplace (Abuela)

TELL A TRICKY TALE

Cloud Weaver (Anansi and the Talking Melon)

Why Elephants Never Forget (Nine-in-One, Grr! Grr!)

Leo's Trip to the City (Coyote)

Rosie Flamingo (Rabbit and Tiger)

TAKE-HOME/KEEP-AT-HOME BOOK

Out of the Blue

Use with "This Is the Way We Go to School."

HARCOURT BRACE & COMPANY

New School, New Friends

by Jared Jansen

"Wasn't school fun, just as I said it would be?" Mrs. Mouse asked.

"It was great," said Mouse.

Mouse sat with his head leaning against his hand. He didn't hear what his mother said next because he was thinking about something else—his next day at school!

Mouse was afraid. He was the only mouse going to the school by the mountain.

"Don't be afraid," his mother said. "Mountain Park School will be fun. If you are nice, the other animals will be nice, too. You will see!"

So Mouse went off. He wanted to get a good start because the school was far away. He was having a nice walk when he heard something. He turned and then jumped back in surprise!

"This is Pony," said Mouse. "He is my new friend from school."

"Hi, Pony," said Mrs. Mouse. "Maybe Mouse can give you a ride to school one day."

Pony laughed and said, "Good joke, Mrs. Mouse." Everyone laughed.

After that, Pony said, "I'll see you in the morning, Mouse."

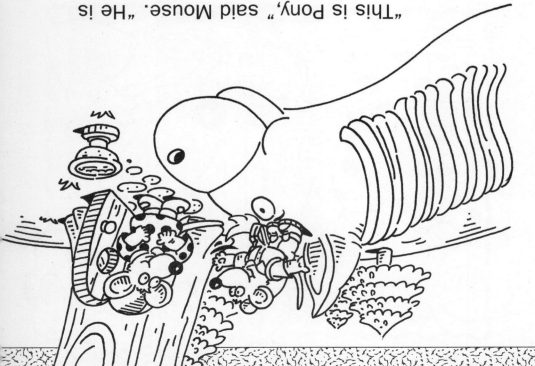

When the teacher came, it was time for school to start. By the end of the day, Mouse liked his teacher and his class a lot. Mouse was almost sorry when school ended. But then he thought of how much fun his ride home with Pony would be.

"Hi," said Pony. "I'm sorry about the noise. It's these new shoes for school. Look at this one."

"Your shoes are nice, but I see what you mean," said Mouse.

"Are you also going to Mountain Park School?" asked Pony.

"Yes," said Mouse.

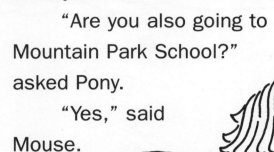

For Mouse, playtime was almost as much fun as his ride. Cub was nice. Mouse liked her. Kitten was nice. Mouse liked her, too. Mouse liked every animal he met.

4

9

"Hop up," said Pony. "I'll give you a ride to school."

"Are you sure?" asked Mouse.

"Sometimes I give rides to my friends," said Pony. "And I think you and I are going to be friends."

8

5

Mouse loved the ride. Pony went fast. Mouse curled up against the wind. The trip was great fun!

When they got to school, Pony said, "We're here! We have a little time to play before school starts."

Mouse got down. He hoped the other animals would be as nice as Pony.

6

7

TAKE-HOME/KEEP-AT-HOME BOOK

Out of the Blue

Use with "Emily and Alice Again."

HARCOURT BRACE & COMPANY

The Case of the Missing Lunch

by Jean Groce

I made Rick a new sandwich. Then I wrote *Case Closed* on my pad while I sang,

"Now you're no longer in a jam.
Aren't you glad you called on Sam?"

12

It was a slow day at the office. There wasn't enough work to do. I needed a case. Something to make me think. Something to make me feel like singing.

Shortly after noon, I heard someone at the door.

1

I put some dog food in a dish in front of Happy. He gave it one sniff and went back to sleep.

"I knew it! He isn't hungry because he's already eaten," I said. "I'm sorry about your sandwich, Rick, but Happy ate it! See the peanut butter on him?"

It was a boy I knew. He looked sad.

"I need your help," he said.

"You've come to the right place!" I sang.

"Got a problem?
Lost your cat?
Sam can find it
just like that!"

I looked around. Soon I had seen what I was looking for.

I ran next door to borrow three things. Then I ran back home.

"I think I know where your sandwich is," I called to Rick. "Watch!"

"Tell me about it," I said, taking out my pen. "First of all, what's your name?"

"You know my name," the boy said. "I'm your brother."

"All the same, you have to tell me your name," I said. "That's how it's done."

"All right," he said. "My name is Rick."
I wrote the name on my pad. "Now,
Rick, tell me your problem," I said.

"My problem is my lunch," Rick said.
"It's gone!"

Rick and I went home. There was the
plate on the table. I gave it a long look. I
didn't see a sandwich.

"I hope you find my sandwich soon,"
Rick said. "I'm hungry!"

I needed an idea, and I needed it fast.

Rick started to laugh. "You know where I eat lunch," he said. "You live in the same house!"

"All the same, you have to take me there. That's how it's done."

8

I wrote *lunch* and *gone* on my pad. "That's not odd," I said. "Lunches are always gone after you eat them."

"I didn't eat it!" Rick said. "I made a big, beautiful sandwich. I went to get a glass of milk. When I came back to the table, the sandwich was gone! Can you help me find my lunch?"

5

"Sure!" I sang.

"In a pickle? In a jam?
The one you need to call is Sam!"

Rick put his hands over his ears. "That
is enough singing!" he said. "Your songs
are too silly!"

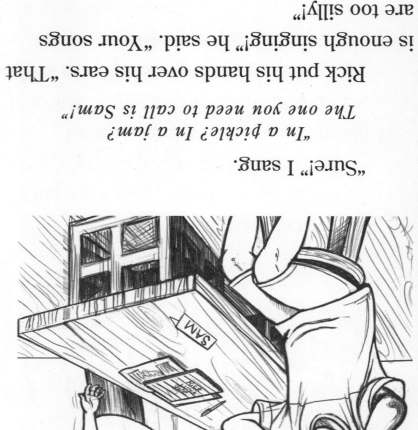

"Sorry," I said. "I always sing. I can't
help it. Anyway, let's go."

"Where are we going?" Rick asked.

"To see your plate," I told him. "Show
me where you eat lunch."

TAKE-HOME/KEEP-AT-HOME BOOK

Out of the Blue

Use with "Max Found Two Sticks."

RUN-AWAY TIRE

HARCOURT BRACE & COMPANY

by Ben Farrell

Then Adam's mother appeared.

"Adam," said Mother, "you were going to see your friends *after* we went to the store. Couldn't you wait?"

Adam saw Mother's smile. He smiled back. Everybody laughed. It had been a long day.

One day, when Mother and Adam were driving to the store, the car made a funny sound—a big **THUMP!**

"Oh no," said Mother. "We have a flat tire. I'll have to fix it."

"Let me help you," said Adam. "I'll get the spare tire." As Adam lifted the tire out of the van, it got away from him. It started to roll down the hill.

Adam watched the tire. He was sure it was going to fall, but it didn't. The tire was getting away!

"Oh, no!" yelled Adam.

Then Mother looked up and saw the tire.

"Oh, no!" she said.

Juan and Tisha were surprised.

"Oh, look, Tisha!" Juan said. "Kerry has brought another tire for us."

"Kerry," Tisha said, laughing, "the tire you brought is too big."

"No more jokes—please!" Kerry said. She and Adam began to laugh, too.

Then Kerry ran even faster. She got close to the tire . . . and stopped it!

"Thanks, Kerry," Adam called. "Thanks very much!"

10

Adam ran after the tire.

"Don't run in the street!" Mother called after him.

Adam ran on. He saw his friend Kerry playing with something.

"Kerry," Adam yelled. "Watch out!"

3

Kerry heard Adam and the sound of
the tire at the same time. She jumped and
got out of the way. The tire ran right over
her puzzle.

"Oh, no!" she said. "I'm going to have
to start all over."

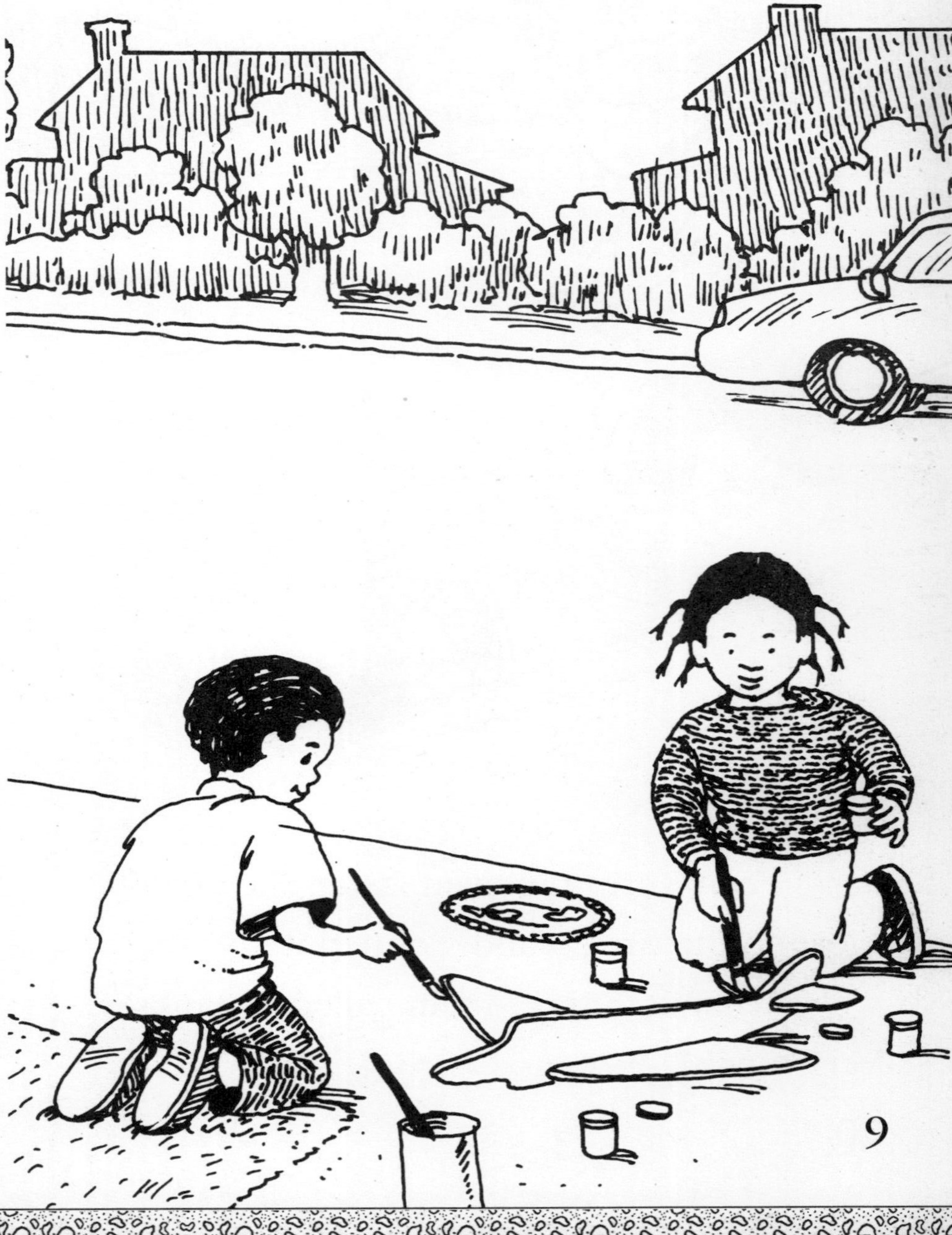

4

9

Adam saw his friends Juan and Tisha. They were making a toy plane. The tire was headed right for them, but Kerry was close to it.

8

5

"Come on, Kerry!" Adam said. "Help me stop that tire before it gets lost."

"I would have gotten the tire," Kerry said, "but you told me to watch out."

"I didn't want the tire to hit you," Adam said.

"Not me!" Kerry said. "I'm fast and strong. Come on! I'll show you." And Kerry began running even faster.

TAKE-HOME/KEEP-AT-HOME BOOK

Out of the Blue

Use with "Dinosaurs Alive and Well!"

HARCOURT BRACE & COMPANY

THE BEST MACHINE

by Susannah Brin

"I have lots of parts," said the car.

"You are a good machine, but I'm a *great* machine because I can think," said the boy.

The car and the boy shook hands. The car knew that the boy was right. The body was, and still is, the best machine.

12

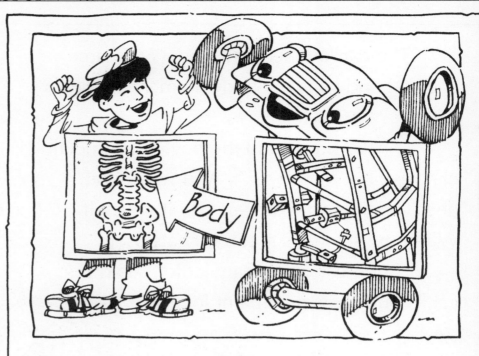

"The car is the best machine in the world," said the car.

"You're wrong. The body is the best machine in the world," said the boy.

"Do you have a frame made of metal?" asked the car.

"No. My frame is made of 206 bones," said the boy.

1

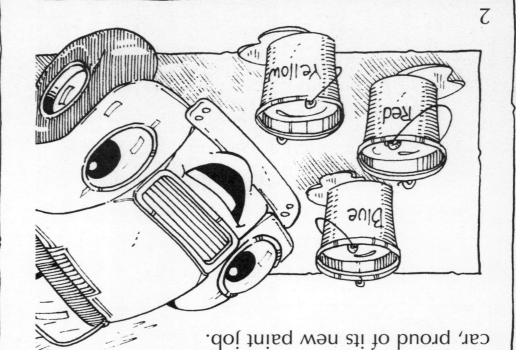

The car laughed and said, "My frame is metal and so is my body. I am very strong."

"I have skin," said the boy. "Your metal can rust, but mine won't. And when you need a paint job, you can't do it yourself. When my skin gets a cut, it heals itself."

"But a car can be any color," said the car, proud of its new paint job.

"I bet you don't have a computer in you like I do," said the car.

"I have a computer that's better than yours," smiled the boy. "I have a brain. My brain does many things. It makes my body move. I use my brain to think and to remember things."

"I'm faster than you," said the car with a grin. "Watch this practice lap!"

"You *are* faster than I am. But when you run out of gas, you won't be able to move," said the boy. "I can walk and run and climb and jump and hop with my feet."

10

3

"And you don't have thumbs," said the boy.

"What do you do with your thumbs?" asked the car.

The boy moved his thumbs. "Thumbs help me pick up things," the boy said.

"I run with gas," said the car.

The boy pointed to his chest. "I have a special muscle that pumps blood to all parts of my body. It is my heart."

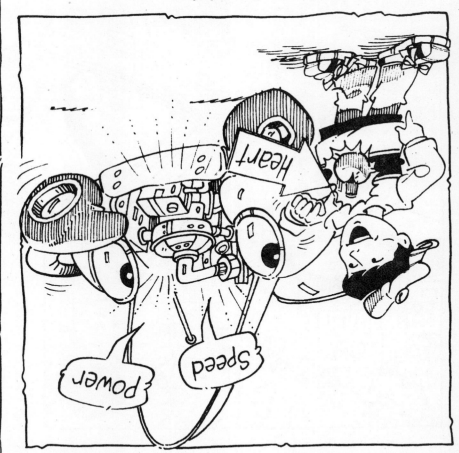

"You have many parts, but you don't have ears," said the boy.

"Why do you need ears?" asked the car.

"I use my ears to hear things. I can hear things that are close by and things that are far away."

8

"I have lights," said the car. "You don't have lights."

"I have eyes to see with," said the boy. "I can see many things."

5

The car began to cry. Big drops of water fell from its wipers. "I bet you can't do this all by yourself," cried the car.

"Yes, I can," said the boy. "I cry when I remember something sad or when I feel bad. When I cry, the water washes my eyes."

"You don't have a grill like mine," shouted the car. The car was starting to get upset.

"You're wrong," said the boy. "I have teeth. My teeth are special. They help me eat things."

6

7

TAKE-HOME/KEEP-AT-HOME BOOK

Out of the Blue
Use with "Matthew and Tilly."

HARCOURT BRACE & COMPANY

SISTERS *Forever*

by Leigh Holliday

"What do you say if all four of us play together sometime?" asked Ana.

"What a good idea—but only if *you* push me on the swing," Marta said.

"It's a deal!" said Ana. "I'll even let you wear my favorite purple hat."

Marta just smiled.

12

Marta loves her sister, Ana. She wants to be just like her when she grows up. She wondered what it would be like to be nine years old, like Ana.

Marta and Ana like to do a lot of things together. They play at the park, eat ice cream, and play games. Sometimes Ana lets Marta put on her favorite purple hat.

1

One day, Ana and Marta were playing at the park.

"Push me harder," said Marta.

Ana was the best at pushing the swing.

"I can't push any harder," said Ana. "I don't want the swing to break, and I don't want you to fall off!"

After a while, Ana's friend from school came by.

"Hi, Ana," said Katie.

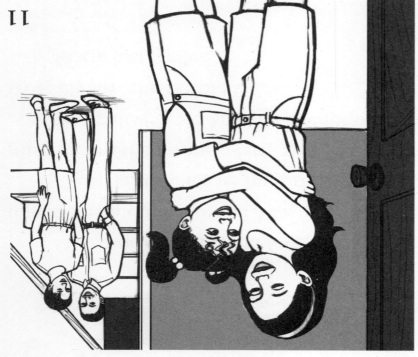

"I missed you while you were gone," said Ana.

"You did?" asked Marta. "I thought you and Katie were having more fun without me."

"Don't be silly, Marta," said Ana. "You are my sister. I like to play with you, too!"

Marta gave Ana a big hug.

"Hi, Marta," said Ana. "I was wondering where you were."

"Mom and I went to the park," said Marta. "I made a new friend. We played games and she shared a cookie with me. She's almost as good as you at pushing the swing!"

10

"Do you want to go play?" Katie asked Ana.

"Sure," said Ana.

"Do you want to come, too, Marta?" asked Katie.

"No, thanks. I'll just play on the swings."

Katie and Ana looked as if they were having fun. Marta felt sorry for herself. She wondered if Ana had more fun with Katie than she did with her.

3

"Your new friend seems very nice," said Mom.

"Oh, yes. We had a good time!" said Marta.

"It's not so bad playing with new friends, is it?" asked Mom.

"You're right, Mom!" said Marta. Then she thought about Ana.

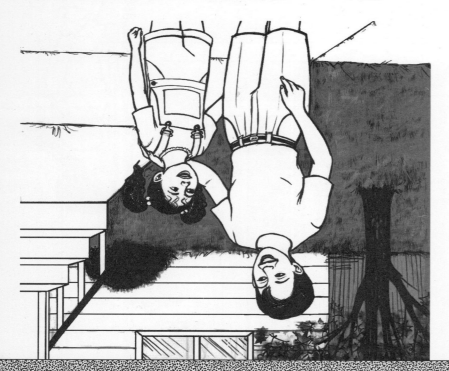

"It's getting late, Katie. I need to get home," said Ana.

Ana waved good-bye to Katie, and she and Marta started to walk home.

"You like Katie, don't you?" asked Marta.

"Yes, she's my friend," Ana said. "Why?"

"Just wondering," said Marta.

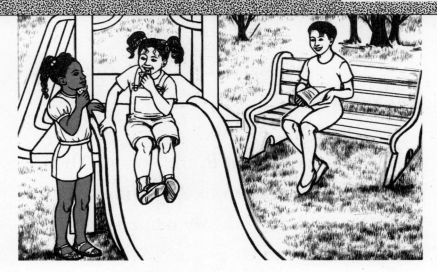

"Do you want to share a cookie with me? I can break it in two for us," said Mindy.

"Yes, thanks!" said Marta.

Marta and Mindy had a lot of fun together. The slide was fun. But they had an even better time playing games.

"It's time to go, Marta," said Mom.

"I hope I'll see you again tomorrow, Mindy," said Marta.

"Me, too!" said Mindy as they waved good-bye.

8

"How was the park?" Dad asked the girls.

"It was fun," said Ana. "My friend Katie was there. Is it okay if she comes over tomorrow?"

"Only after your homework is done," said Mom as she handed her a piece of pie.

"Would you like a piece of pie, Marta?" asked Mom.

"No, thanks," Marta said.

Marta thought about Ana and Katie playing together. She began to feel sorry for herself again.

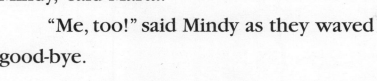

5

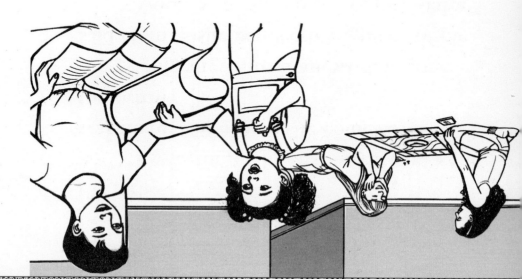

"Come on, Marta. Let's go to the park," said Mom.

"Okay," Marta said.

Marta went right to the swings. Then she saw a girl walk up to the swings.

"Hi," said the girl. "My name is Mindy."

"Hi, I'm Marta."

"Want to play on the slide with me?" asked Mindy.

"Yes!" said Marta.

The next day, Katie came over to play. Marta watched as Katie and Ana had a good time together. Marta played by herself. Then she went to talk to Mom.

"What's the matter, Marta?" asked Mom.

"All Ana wants to do is play with Katie. Why doesn't she want to play with me?"

"Ana still loves to play with you. But sometimes it's fun to play with other friends, too," said Mom.

TAKE-HOME/KEEP-AT-HOME BOOK

Out of the Blue

Use with "Mr. Putter and Tabby Pour the Tea."

THE PERFECT PET

by Jessica Jansen

HARCOURT BRACE & COMPANY

"Oh, what a surprise!" Mark said. "I never would have guessed a turtle."

"Yes," said Latasha, "this is a big surprise. Now I'm sure your pet isn't going to be loud."

"I see the turtle's head!" Kim said. "Oh, now I get it. The turtle's head goes in and out of its shell without Mrs. Green's help. We were all tricked!"

"My new pet will be perfect company for me," said Mrs. Green, "just like you kids are!"

12

Mark, Kim, and Latasha were friends. They went to school together. And after school, they walked their dogs together. They enjoyed each other's company.

1

One day, Mark said, "I think Mrs. Green is going to get a dog."

Mark's friends looked surprised.

"Are you sure?" asked Kim.

"Yes," Mark went on. "I saw a man from the Best Pet Shop at Mrs. Green's house. He was talking with her for a long time."

The man from the Best Pet Shop came the next day. Mark, Kim, and Latasha saw him at Mrs. Green's door. They waited until he was gone. Then they went to see Mrs. Green.

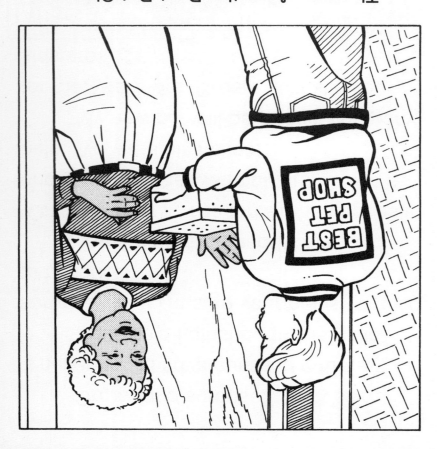

 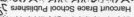

Another day went by. "Mrs. Green can't trick *me*," Latasha said. "Her little pet doesn't eat much because it's just a baby animal. I'm sure it's a kitten. Kittens are very quiet."

10

"A pet, maybe," Latasha said, "but not a dog. Mrs. Green once told me that she used to have a dog. She said she never enjoyed having a dog for a pet because she didn't like walking it all the time."

"A pet sure would keep her company," said Mark.

3

"A cat would be a wonderful pet for Mrs. Green," said Kim. "Does she like cats?"

"I don't know," Latasha said. "Let's go ask Mrs. Green about her pet, but let's take our dogs home first. Mrs. Green can do without three children *and* three dogs."

A day later, Mark said, "I've been thinking about Mrs. Green's pet. It must be a hamster. That's my guess. A hamster is little and doesn't eat a lot. A hamster would be a wonderful pet for Mrs. Green."

The children enjoyed guessing what Mrs. Green's pet would be. Kim said, "I think Mrs. Green's new pet will be a little bird."

A bird would go in and out of its cage without help.

Mrs. Green said, "Yes, I will have a new pet in four days. But I'm not going to tell you what it is. I'll give you some hints. Then you take turns guessing what it is while you walk your dogs."

"I'm sure I'll guess what your pet will be," Kim said.

"I picked a pet that doesn't make a lot of loud noise," Mrs. Green said. "My new pet is going to be perfect company. It's little, and it doesn't eat a lot. One last thing—the pet can go in and out without me. Now have fun guessing!"

TAKE-HOME/KEEP-AT-HOME BOOK

Out of the Blue

Use with "Six-Dinner Sid."

HARCOURT BRACE & COMPANY

THE BIG SNEEZE

by Jean Groce

Uncle Chase left to go find a mouse. "Thanks, friend," said Miles. "That was close! I came within a whisker of being a snack for your Uncle Chase!"

"That was *too* close!" Tabby said. "In the future, hold your breath when you feel a sneeze coming!"

Tabby was a city cat. If he had been a farm cat, maybe things would have been different. Maybe he would have been brought up to catch mice.

But no. Tabby was a city cat who was always looking for new friends. That's how he discovered Miles.

Uncle Chase jumped. Tabby jumped, too. He jumped so fast that he almost sat on top of Miles.

Tabby covered his mouth. "Excuse me," he said. "Drinking milk always makes me sneeze."

Miles was a mouse who lived in the same building as Tabby. One day, Miles was looking for something good for his dinner.

At the same time, Tabby was going out for his afternoon walk. He wasn't watching where he was going. BAM! Tabby and Miles met.

Then a very bad thing happened. Miles felt a sneeze coming. A very BIG sneeze. He held it in and held it in, but then . . .

"Ah—ah—aaaah—CHOO!"

10

"Sorry," said Tabby. "Here, let me help you up."

"Help me up?" said Miles. "Aren't you going to eat me?"

"Why would I want to eat you?" Tabby asked. "You live here, don't you? That means we're neighbors. Even if I caught you, I wouldn't eat you. Neighbors don't eat each other."

3

Miles dusted off his tail. "I've always heard that cats eat mice," he said. He tried to smile in a friendly way, but it's hard to smile when you're a mouse and you've just bumped into a cat.

Tabby laughed. "That's just a funny idea some people and some cats have," he said. "I think mice are nice."

"That?" asked Tabby, thinking fast. "That's just a . . . a . . . a toy mouse! Just my little toy mouse. It looks just like the real thing. It even smells like the real thing!"

"Hmmmm," said Uncle Chase as he scratched his chin. "They didn't make toys like that when I was a kitten." He put his big cat nose close to Miles's whiskers. Miles didn't move.

Miles lay down. He tried to look very small.

"Mmmmm!" Uncle Chase said. "I smell something good. Isn't that . . . a mouse?"

"Oh, no," said Tabby. "That's just my milk and crackers. I was having a snack."

Then Uncle Chase spotted Miles. "There!" he cried. "I *knew* I smelled a mouse!"

8

That's how Tabby and Miles became friends. They were together almost every day.

Sometimes they played ball.
Sometimes they played hide-and-seek.

Tabby scratched Miles's back where Miles couldn't reach. Miles scratched Tabby's back where Tabby couldn't reach. They had discovered how nice it was to be friends.

5

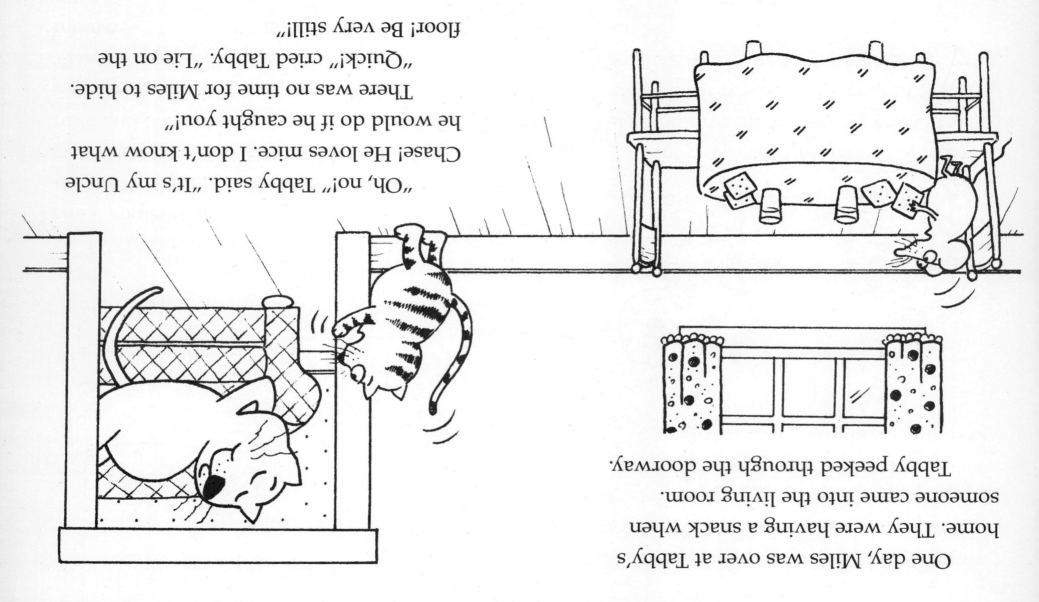

One day, Miles was over at Tabby's home. They were having a snack when someone came into the living room. Tabby peeked through the doorway.

"Oh, no!" Tabby said. "It's my Uncle Chase! He loves mice. I don't know what he would do if he caught you!"

There was no time for Miles to hide. "Quick!" cried Tabby. "Lie on the floor! Be very still!"

TAKE-HOME/KEEP-AT-HOME BOOK
Out of the Blue
Use with "Abuela."

HARCOURT BRACE & COMPANY

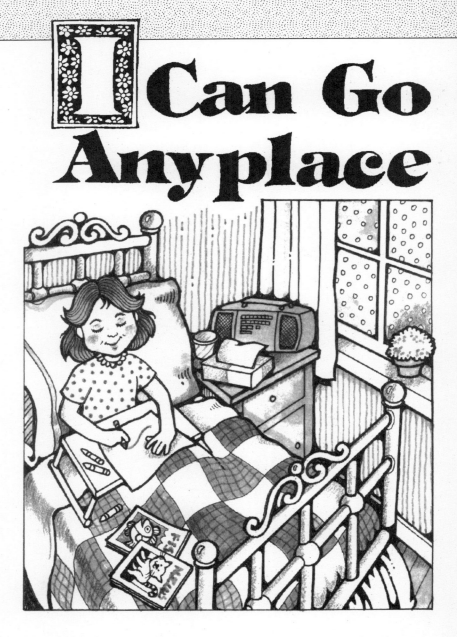

I Can Go Anyplace

by T. Ernesto Bethancourt

I get back to my room just in time. Mom comes in and says, "Time for dinner, Jenny. You have been so good today. I'm sorry if you didn't have much fun."

"I had a great time," I say. She may never know what adventures I have had!

Tomorrow, if I'm still sick, I may fly to the moon!

12

My name is Jenny. I can't go to school today with my cousin, Linda, because I have a cold. I have to stay in bed. I can only read my books or draw pictures.

"That doesn't sound like fun," you might say. Well, not at all. I close my eyes and have an adventure! I can go anyplace I want.

1

I make believe my bed can fly, and I go across the country. I go to the mountains and play in the snow. My bed becomes a sled. Snow is cold to touch, but not for me. I'm as warm as I can be in my sled bed. Down the mountain I go, flying over the snow.

2

11

I am ready for my next adventure. I go to the sea, and my bed turns into a sub. I am under the water.

I go through the water looking at all the sea life. I see bright blue fish, beautiful shells, and even a big shark.

I like being under the water.

10

I also make believe that my bed is a boat. The people on the other boats are surprised to see my bed boat.

The fish and the birds play games with me. The fish jump over my bed while the birds fly all around.

3

6

When I'm not sailing on the water, my bed becomes a train. I can make the whole train go fast or slow. I am the person on the train who says, "All aboard!" I smile at the people who get on my train.

4

My bed car grows wings and becomes a plane. "Welcome aboard," I say to the people who get on the plane.

I fly us high in the sky and over a tall building. Then I see the President!

"Hello, Mr. President," I say as I fly over. He sees me and waves.

I keep flying across the country. Then I land my plane and the people get off. I say, "Thank you for flying Jenny Airlines!"

"Time for lunch, Jenny," my mom says. The train and tracks go away.

She brings me food on a tray. I'm hungry because I've been so many places in one day. I eat my lunch right away, for I have more places to go.

7

Sometimes, a horse does not go as fast as I want to go. I pretend that my bed is a race car and that I am at a big racetrack. I pass a red car, then a blue car. "Jenny wins!" the whole crowd yells. I don't stop, for I have other places to go.

6

Mom takes my tray away, and my bed becomes a horse and wagon. Now I'm on a cowgirl adventure! My horse pulls my bed wagon faster and faster. "Yippee!" I cry.

TAKE-HOME/KEEP-AT-HOME BOOK
Out of the Blue
Use with "Anansi and the Talking Melon."

Did you know that the
word for spider and cloud
is the same in Japanese?
The word is *kumo*.

HARCOURT BRACE & COMPANY

Cloud Weaver

retold by Susannah Brin

Mr. Sato went back to his yard and looked up at the sky. He saw a fluffy, white cloud that looked like cotton.

"Spider is up in the sky," said Mr. Sato. He didn't know how she had climbed so high, but he knew she had made the fluffy cloud.

Today, in Japan, when people see fluffy clouds, they say they are the work of the Spider-Girl.

12

Long ago, in Japan, there was a farmer named Mr. Sato. One day, he saw a spider web with a spider in it. The spider was beautiful!

Mr. Sato said, "I'm glad to have you in my garden." Then he saw a hungry lizard walking over to the spider.

"Oh, no!" Mr. Sato said. The spider hid, and Mr. Sato chased the lizard away. This made the lizard angry.

1

When Mr. Sato was chasing the lizard, he ripped his robe on a thorn. Mr. Sato looked at his torn robe. It could not be fixed.

"I don't know how I can get another robe," he said.

The spider looked for a place to hide. She saw a ray of sun and this gave her an idea. She started to make a web. Running and spinning, she climbed her web all the way to the sky.

Mr. Sato didn't see the spider. But he did see the lizard, and he chased it from his yard.

Mr. Sato put the cotton by the door where the spider was working. When he woke up in the morning, he peeked in the window and saw the spider. She had used up most of the cotton.

Then he saw the lizard in the room! The spider saw the lizard, too. She jumped out the window, and the lizard ran after her.

10

That night, Mr. Sato heard someone knocking. He put on his robe and went to the door. A girl was there. Her robe looked like something he had seen before, but he couldn't remember what it was.

The girl said, "You need a new robe. Would you like me to make one for you?"

"Yes, of course!" said Mr. Sato.

3

The girl wanted to get to work. So Mr. Sato showed her to the next room. There was a large basket of cotton in the room. Then Mr. Sato went back to his room and fell asleep.

When Mr. Sato woke up, he was very surprised. Seven new robes were next to his mat.

6

Mr. Sato left the window. He would keep the spider's secret. The next day, he went to town and got more cotton for the spider.

On his way back home he got tired and he stopped to rest.

The angry lizard saw him. "I will go with him and look for the spider," said the lizard.

The lizard got into the cart and hid in the cotton.

Mr. Sato didn't see the girl. He only saw a spider. Then it came to him. The girl had changed into a spider. And she looked like the spider from his garden—the one he had saved from the lizard!

"The spider must not be hungry because she is full of cotton," he thought. He watched the spider as she ate the cotton and then used it to spin out thread.

8

"You have used the cotton to make these beautiful robes," said Mr. Sato. "One for each day of the week. How can I thank you?"

"I have only one wish," said the girl.

"Of course. What is it?" asked Mr. Sato.

"Please do not come into the room while I am working," said the girl.

5

7

Mr. Sato wanted to know what was going on in the room where the girl worked.

"Maybe I should bore a hole in the door and take a peek," he said. No, he would peek in the window. So he squeezed himself between a tree and the wall of the house. Then he looked in the window.

Every night, Mr. Sato put a plate of food at the door of the room. But the girl didn't eat the food.

"She must be hungry," he said to himself. But he didn't open the door.

Every morning, Mr. Sato found new robes by his mat. "I'm sure of one thing—she is not lazy," he said as he looked at the robes.

TAKE-HOME/KEEP-AT-HOME BOOK
Out of the Blue
Use with "Nine-in-One, Grr! Grr!"

WHY ELEPHANTS NEVER FORGET

by Meish Goldish

HARCOURT BRACE & COMPANY

Elephant felt terrible about what she had done.

"I guess I don't remember well," she sighed. "But what can I do about it?"

Zebra said, "I know. Go to the Animal King with us. Tell him that your wish is to always remember things!"

And that's just what Elephant did.

And that's why, today, they say an elephant never forgets!

12

They say that an elephant never forgets. Do you know why? Here's a story that tells you.

Long ago, in a place far away, all the animals of the world lived together. No two animals looked the same. Yet each animal wanted to change its looks in some way.

1

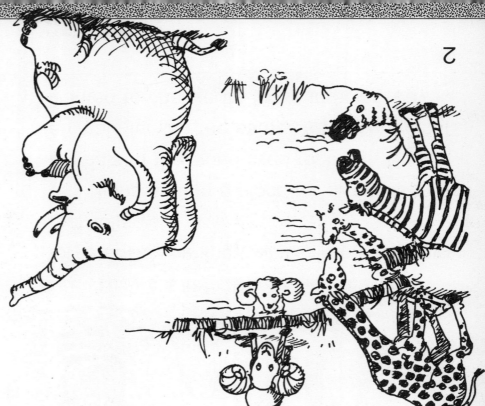

"My neck is long," said Giraffe. "But I want an even longer neck."

"I have stripes," said Zebra. "But I want even more stripes."

"My horns are big," sighed Sheep. "But I want even bigger horns."

Elephant heard each animal's wish.

All the animals ran to Elephant.

"What did you do to us?" they shouted. "We look terrible!"

"I . . . I'm sorry," Elephant said. "I told Animal King your wishes. I guess I didn't remember them the right way."

"No, you didn't," Giraffe sighed. "And now look at us! Now we must all go to Animal King to see if he can change us back again."

Elephant began the walk home. After many days, she was almost there. But as she came close, she heard a funny noise. It came from her animal friends. Then Elephant saw them. How funny they all looked!

10

"My shell is hard," said Turtle. "But I want an even harder shell."

"I have a hump," sighed Camel. "But I want more humps."

"I have spots," said Leopard. "But I want even more spots."

All the animals turned to Elephant. "What do *you* wish for?" they asked.

"I don't know," said Elephant. "I will have to think about it."

3

Far from this place lived Animal King. He was very important. Everybody knew Animal King could change an animal's looks.

The animals decided to go see Animal King. "We can all tell him our wishes," they said.

"Animal King lives very far away," said Turtle. "Only one of us should go. One of us can tell Animal King all our wishes."

4

It was important for Elephant to remember each animal's wish. After a long time, she said, "Now I remember! Giraffe wants a harder shell. Zebra wants more spots. Sheep wants more stripes. Turtle wants a longer neck. Camel wants bigger horns. And Leopard wants more humps."

"Are you sure?" Animal King asked.

"Yes," Elephant said.

"So be it!" Animal King said.

6

Elephant walked
a long way to the home of
Animal King. The trip was long
and lonely. But after many days, she
got there. Animal King was outside.

"Hello, Elephant," said Animal King.
"What are you doing here?"

"I have come to tell you the wishes of
all my friends," explained Elephant as she
handed him the coins.

"And what are their wishes?" asked
Animal King.

8

"That's a good idea," said Sheep.
"Yes," said Camel. "But which one of us
should go?"

"I think Elephant should go," said
Zebra. "Elephant doesn't know what to
wish for. Maybe on her way to Animal King,
she will think of something."

"That's a good idea!" all the animals
decided.

5

Everyone turned to Elephant. "Do you remember each of our wishes?" they asked.

"Yes," said Elephant. "Giraffe wants a longer neck. Zebra wants more stripes. Sheep wants bigger horns. Turtle wants a harder shell. Camel wants more humps. And Leopard wants more spots."

"We will need to pay Animal King," said Giraffe. So they each gave some coins to Elephant.

"Be sure to tell Animal King what we each wish for," said Zebra. "It's very important."

"I will," said Elephant. And she set off on her way.

6

7

TAKE-HOME/KEEP-AT-HOME BOOK

Out of the Blue

Use with "Coyote."

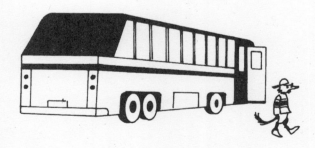

HARCOURT BRACE & COMPANY

LEO'S Trip to the City

by Jeanette Mara

Leo gave his backpack to Cousin Fox. His father had been right. Cousin Fox was trouble, all right—lots of trouble. But Leo had "out foxed" Cousin Fox. Leo still had all his money in his pocket. And he knew he could get his backpack later from Cousin Fox.

12

"The city will be fun, Leo," Father Coyote said. "But watch out for Cousin Fox. He's full of tricks and trouble."

Leo gave his dad a hug and got on the bus.

1

After the bus started, Leo took his
money out of his backpack. He put his
money in his pocket. "This is a good place
to keep it," Leo thought. "It will be safer in
my pocket," he said.

"No!" said Cousin Fox. "I said I
balance a feather on a foot. But I get
to pick the foot. So it looks like I win."
Leo took another look at Bear. "You
win, all right," Leo said.

"Bear, please come here!" Cousin Fox
called. A big bear walked out.

"This coyote thinks he can balance a
feather on your foot," Cousin Fox said.

"I don't think so," said Bear.

"I meant *my* foot!" said Leo.

10

In the city, Leo saw
Cousin Fox. He was
playing with a ball. A
big grin spread across
Cousin Fox's face
when he saw Leo.

"Hi, Cousin
Coyote," he called.
"Come over here."

3

"Can you balance a ball on your head like this?" Cousin Fox asked.

"Sure," Leo said.

"This feather won't be hard for me to balance."

"If you can't balance it, I get your backpack," Cousin Fox said.

Leo laughed at Cousin Fox.

"Sure," Leo told him, "you can have my backpack."

"Good," Cousin Fox said. "I'll hold your backpack while you're doing the trick."

4

9

"I don't think you can balance a feather on a foot," Cousin Fox said.

Leo thought of what his father had said about Cousin Fox. Leo did not want to be foolish.

"Are you talking about a great big feather?" asked Leo.

"No," said Cousin Fox.

"Are you talking about a very little feather?" asked Leo.

"No," said Cousin Fox, "I'm talking about the feather I just used."

8

"I don't think so," Cousin Fox said. "But I'll let you try."

Then he handed the ball to Leo. In one fast move, Leo set the ball on his head.

"Like this?" Leo asked.

5

"Very good work," Cousin Fox said.

"Thanks," said Leo.

Then he took the ball off his head and handed it back to Cousin Fox.

"Cousin Coyote," he said, "it was foolish of me to think you couldn't balance that ball."

7

Cousin Fox took out a feather.

"Watch *this* trick," he said. Leo watched.

"I can do that," Leo said.

"I know," Cousin Fox said, laughing. "Everybody can balance a feather like this. What about doing it on a foot?"

"What about it?" asked Leo.

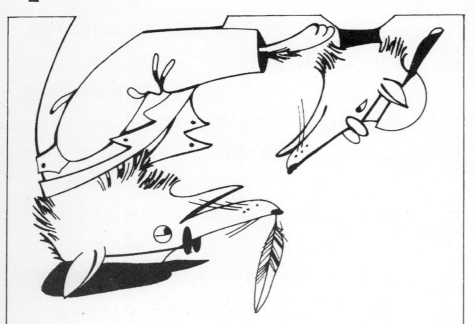

TAKE-HOME/KEEP-AT-HOME BOOK

Out of the Blue

Use with "Rabbit and Tiger."

HARCOURT BRACE & COMPANY

Rosie Flamingo

by Jean Groce

Well, now that I've told you a few things about flamingos, I'd better fly back home. Pinkie will be looking for me!
So long!

12

Hello there!
I'm here to tell
you a few things about
a kind of bird that is
very beautiful. *Me!*
I'm a flamingo—a Greater Flamingo, to be exact. You can call me Rosie.

1

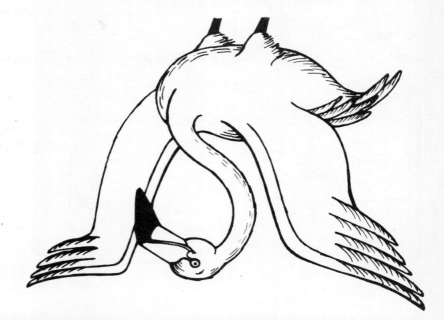

I just landed here in your book. I hope you don't mind. It was a long trip from my home in South America, but I'm good at flying.

See these wings? Very nice, aren't they? Their color is rosy white, and that's where I get my name, Rosie. My bill is pink, too. Let me tell you about it.

Never mind. I'll make another bargain with you. Don't make fun of *my* knees, and I won't make fun of yours. All right?

It scares me to think of how you would look with legs and knees like mine!

Take a look at these legs! They may be thin, but they are just right for walking in water. My body stays nice and dry. See how my knees bend? It seems to me that your knees are kind of funny. They don't bend the right way.

10

My bill is very handy when I want to eat. You see, I live next to a lake near the jungle. I'm happy to tell you that flamingos are not the fiercest kind of bird. We are the kind of bird that likes to eat tiny plants and animals we find in the lake.

3

About five days after
hatching, Pinkie could leave
the nest. By the time she
was a few weeks old, she
could find her own food.

Could *you* walk when
you were five days old?
No, I guess not. But then,
you don't have long legs
like ours.

4

9

The egg hatches after about a month. I'm sure you would like to see a picture of my little girl. Here she is!

Her name is Pinkie. Isn't she cute? She still has her white and gray baby feathers, but her bill was pink right from the start.

8

When I'm hungry, I wade into the water, put my head down, and turn my head upside down. Then I open my mouth, let some water in, and push the water out. The tiny plants and animals left in my mouth are for me to eat.

So whenever I am hungry, I just reach down into the water for a bite to eat. What a bargain!

5

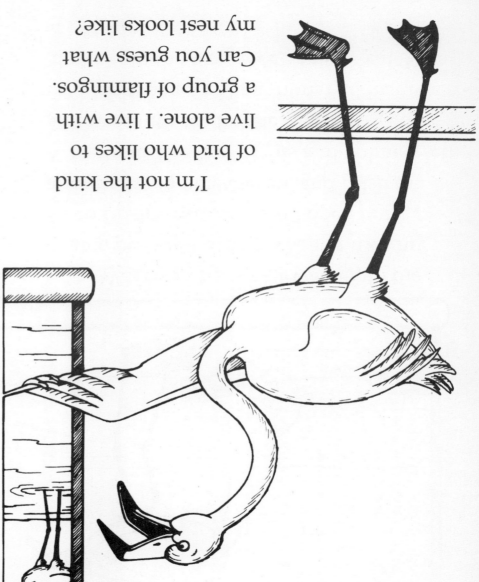

I'm not the kind
of bird who likes to
live alone. I live with
a group of flamingos.
Can you guess what
my nest looks like?

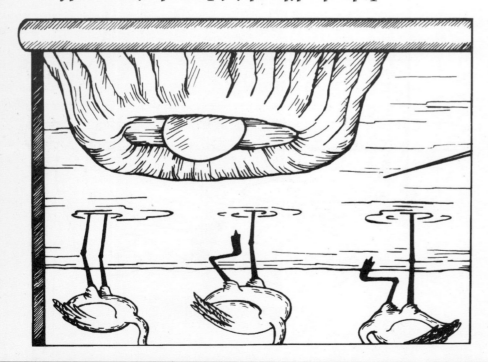

It looks like this! I made it myself
with mud from the bottom of the lake.
There's a place for me to lay my egg.
While the egg lies there, I sit on it to keep
it warm. Mr. Flamingo takes turns sitting
on it, too.

That's what we flamingos call "baby
sitting"!